ELENA FIRSOVA

THREE POEMS BY OSIP MANDELSTAM

Voice and Piano

Boosey & Hawkes Music Publishers Ltd.
Sole Selling Agents of Anglo-Soviet Music Press, London
for Great Britain, Eire and the British Commonwealth (except Canada)

Le Chant du Monde, Paris
pour La France, Belgique, Luxembourg et les Pays francophone de l'Afrique

Edition Fazer, Helsinki
for Finland

G. Ricordi & C., Milano
per l'Italia

Musikverlag Hans Sikorski, Hamburg
*für die Bundesrepublik Deutschland und West-Berlin, Dänemark, Island, Norwegen,
Schweden, Niederlande, Schweiz, Spanien, Portugal, Griechenland, Türkei und Israel*

Universal Edition A.G., Wien
für Österreich

Zen-On Music Company Ltd., Tokyo
for Japan

duration: ca. 9 minutes

Ed. 3843

First Printing: September, 1991

G. SCHIRMER, Inc.

Distributed by
Hal Leonard Publishing Corporation
7777 West Bluemound Road P.O. Box 3819 Milwaukee, WI 53213

Regarding the translation

Mandelstam's great gift as a poet is his ability to create impression-istic, at times almost mystical, effects with very simple Russian words. While these words are often quite long, however, their English equivalents are normally much shorter. A very literal translation would therefore require many melismas where Firsova sets one note per syllable; it would also require tortured syntax to get the key words into positions that make musical sense. I know—I tried.

So—with apologies to the literary scholars who will never forgive me—I have gone for the right feeling where an exact translation proved too intractable, and this has tended to mean elaborating (judiciously, I hope) on the images evoked in the Russian text. The key words in the English do *not* always occur in the same position as their Russian counterparts, but I believe they do occur in places that make musical sense.

I have tried—not always successfully—to use sequences of vowels close in effect to those of the original Russian; where divergence has proved necessary I have avoided using a vowel that is more difficult to sing. I own one totally unfair demand on the singer in my translation: the arrangement of "far-off" at the end of the second song. But I did not choose that rendering until I had made sure I could sing it myself by prolonging the high A in head voice as marked (better, I think, to try to stick to Firsova's original note length, spinning it out *al niente,* but that is beyond my vocal technique.) For a better understanding of the poems, I have also included a poetic translation in the preface.

—GRAHAM HOBBS

Why is [my] soul so songful
And why are there so few dear names,
And the momentary rhythm—is it only chance.
An unexpected Aquila?

It will raise a cloud of dust,
Will rustle in the papery foliage
And not return at all, or
Return completely different.

*Oh wide wind of Orpheus,
  You will depart for ocean regions;
  And, lisping an uncreated world,
  I have forgotten about the unnecessary "I."

I roamed in a whimsical grove
And discovered an azure grotto...
Am I actually real,
And will death indeed come?

Tenderer than tender
Is your face,
Whiter than white
Is your hand,
From the whole world,
You are remote,
And all that is yours,
From the inevitable.

[Remote] From the inevitable
Is your grief
And the fingers of [your]
Uncooling hands
And the soft sound
Of undespairing
Talk
And the distance
Of your eyes.

—OSIP MANDELSTAM
translated by GRAHAM HOBBS

* Firsova did not set this verse.

THREE POEMS BY
OSIP MANDELSTAM

I

Andante con moto

ELENA FIRSOVA

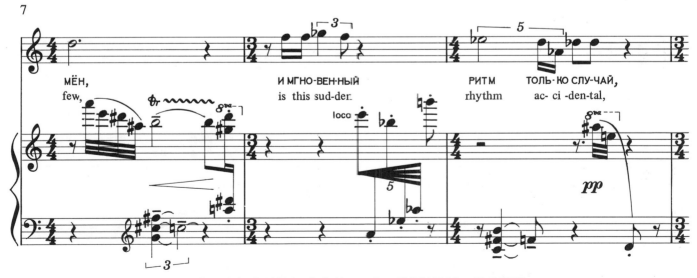

10

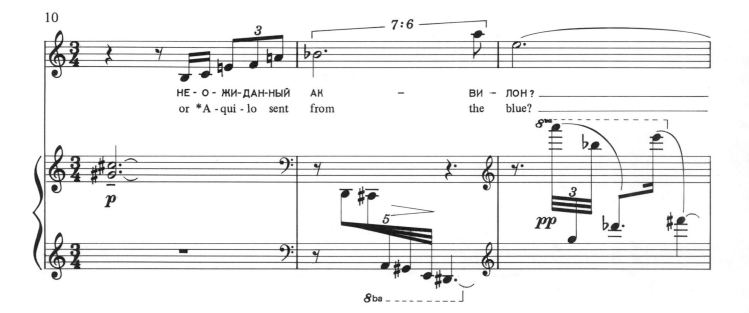

НЕ - О - ЖИ-ДАН-НЫЙ АК — ВИ - ЛОН? _____
or *A - qui - lo sent from the blue? _____

13

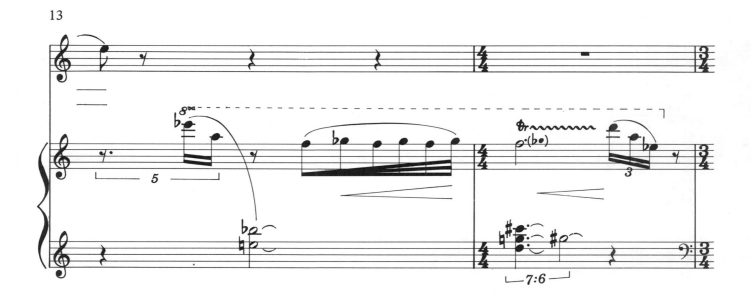

15 **Poco più mosso**

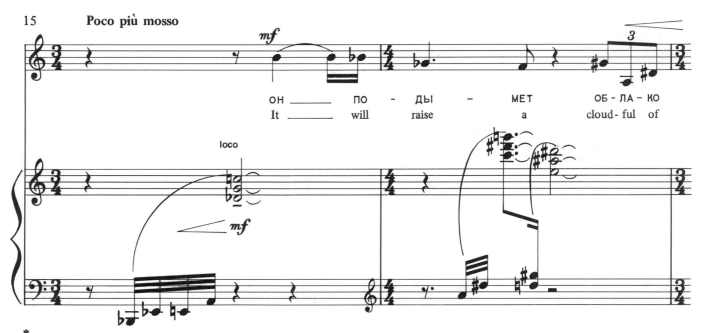

ОН _____ ПО - ДЫ - МЕТ ОБ - ЛА - КО
It _____ will raise a cloud- ful of

* Aquilo (Aquilonis) latin, strong north or north - east wind.

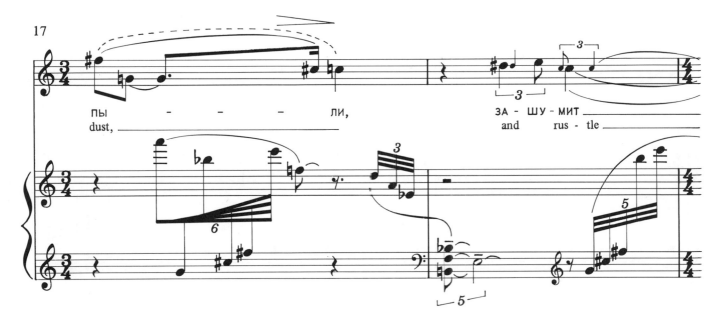

ПЫ - - - ЛИ,   ЗА - ШУ - МИТ
dust,   and rus - tle

БУ - МАЖ - НОЙ ЛИСТ - ВОЙ,
the pa - per - y leaves,

Poco meno mosso

И СОВ - СЕМ НЕ ВЕР-НЁТ-СЯ   И -ЛИ
Ne - ver once will re -turn, or   may - be

* sul corda

* ♪ indicates to pluck the string inside the piano.

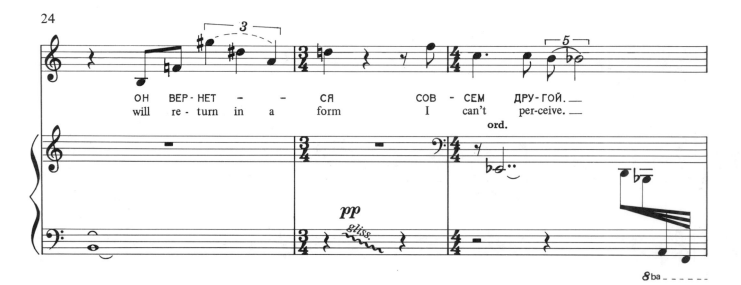

ОН ВЕР - НЕТ - - СЯ СОВ - СЕМ ДРУ - ГОЙ.
will re - turn in a form I can't per-ceive.

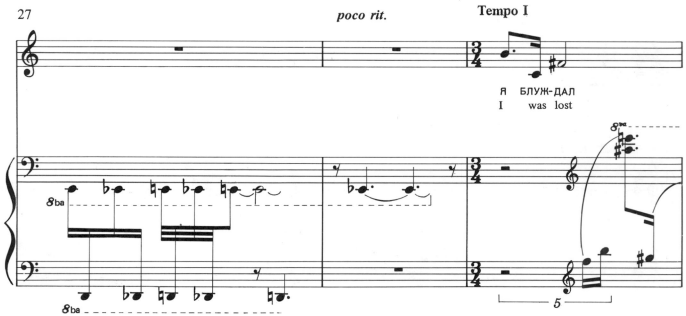

Я БЛУЖ-ДАЛ
I was lost

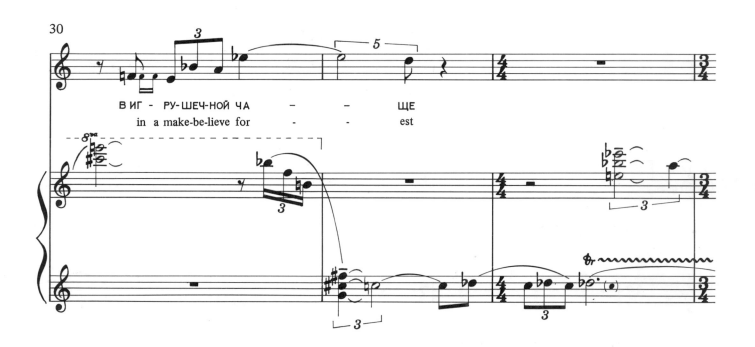

В ИГ - РУ-ШЕЧ-НОЙ ЧА - - ЩЕ
in a make-be-lieve for - - est

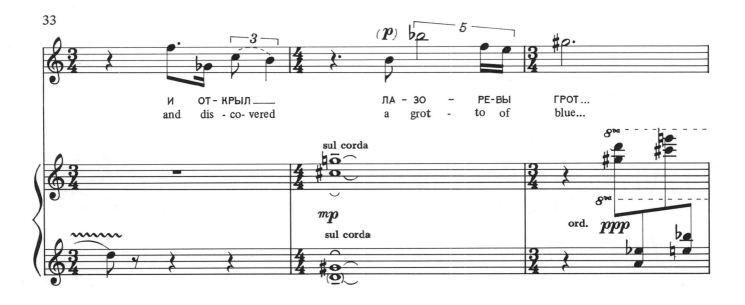

И ОТ - КРЫЛ _____ ЛА - ЗО - РЕ - ВЫ ГРОТ...
and dis - co- vered a grot - to of blue...

НЕ - У - ЖЕ - ЛИ Я НАС-ТО-Я - ЩИЙ, И ДЕЙСТ-
Am I real - ly real, — sub-stan - tial, will death

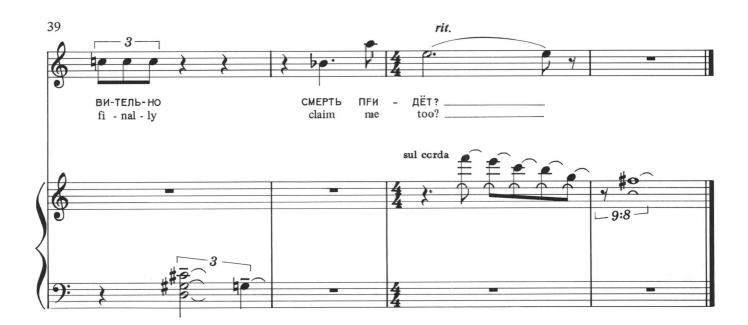

ВИ-ТЕЛЬ-НО СМЕРТЬ ПРИ - ДЁТ? _____
fi - nal - ly claim me too? _____

II

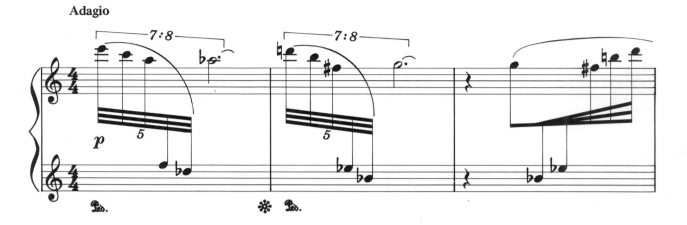

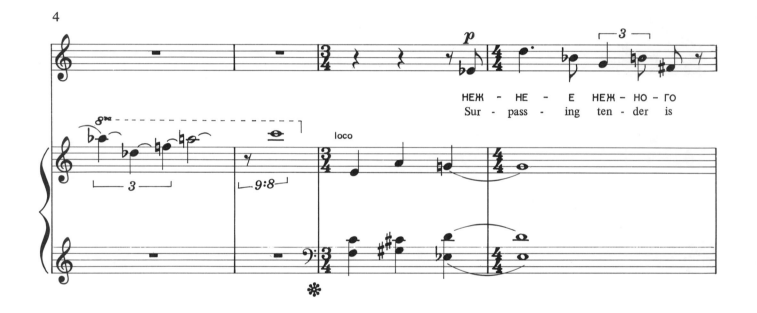

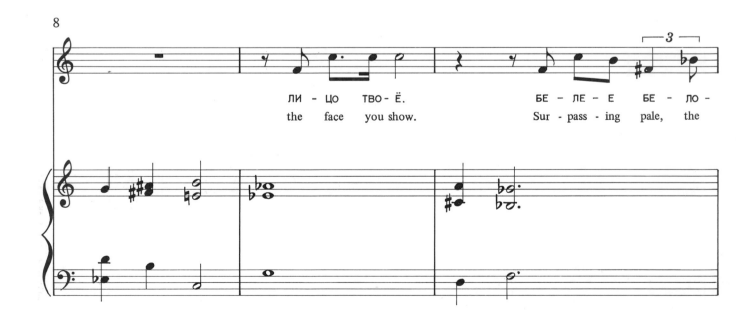

НЕЖ – НЕ – Е НЕЖ – НО – ГО
Sur – pass – ing ten – der is

ЛИ – ЦО ТВО – Ё.
the face you show.

БЕ – ЛЕ – Е БЕ – ЛО –
Sur – pass – ing pale, the

ГО   ТВО - Я РУ - КА.   ОТ МИ - РА ЦЕ - ЛО -
hand   that smoothes the brow   Noth - ing can tres - pass

ГО   ТЫ ДА - ЛЕ - КА   И ВСЁ ТВО - Ё
on   where you are now -   Not all the world

ОТ НЕ - ИЗ - БЕЖ - НО - ГО.
Nor the in - es - cap - a - ble.

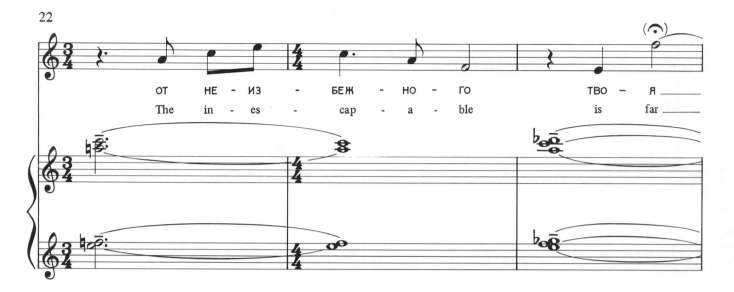

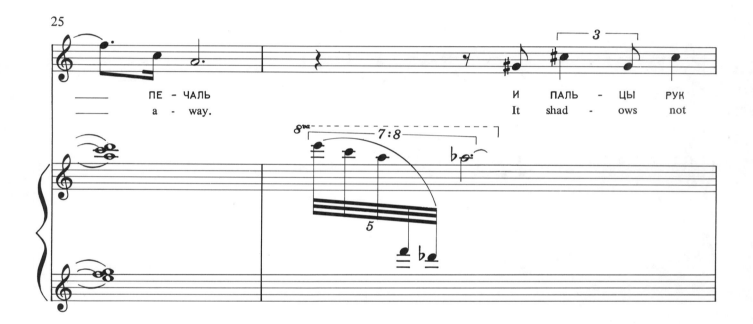

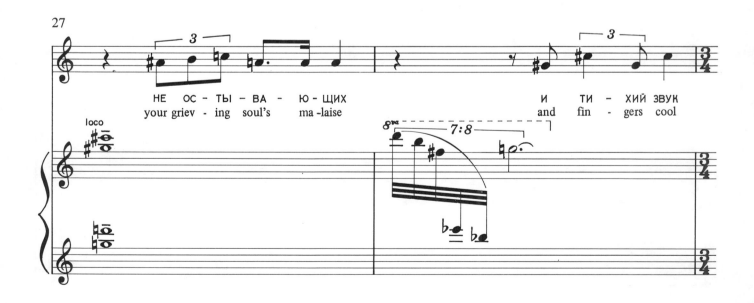

НЕ – У – НЫ – ВА – Ю – ЩИХ РЕ – ЧЕЙ И
and voice un - yield - ing des - pair and

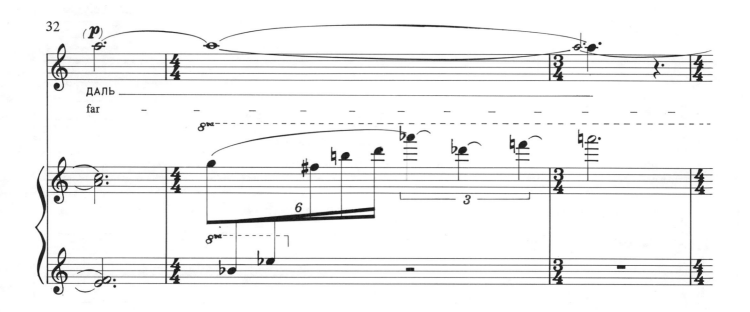

ДАЛЬ _____
far – – – – – – – – – – – –

ТВО – ИХ О – ЧЕЙ.
– – – – off, dis - tant gaze.

III

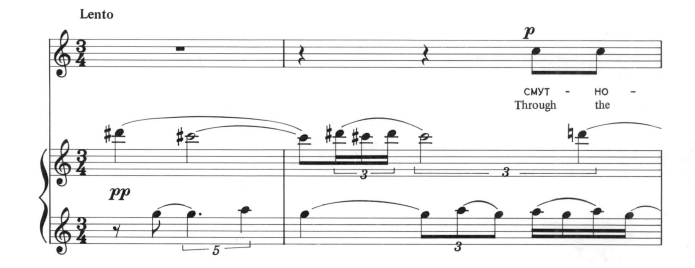

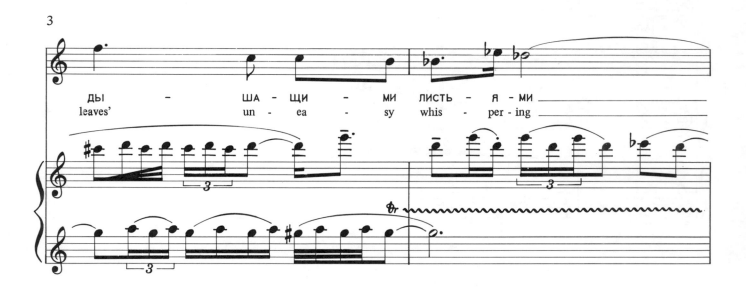

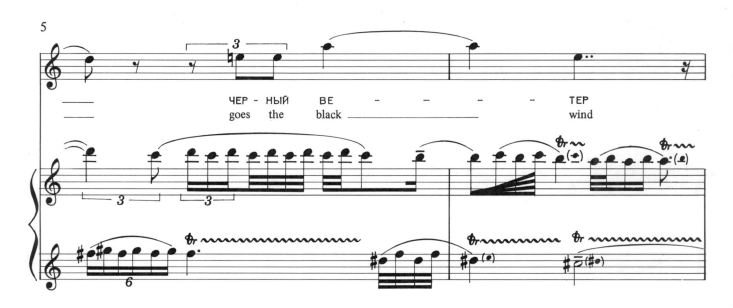

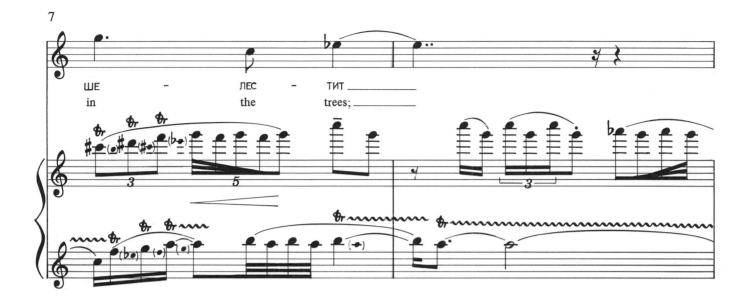

ШЕ - ЛЕС - ТИТ _____
in the trees; _____

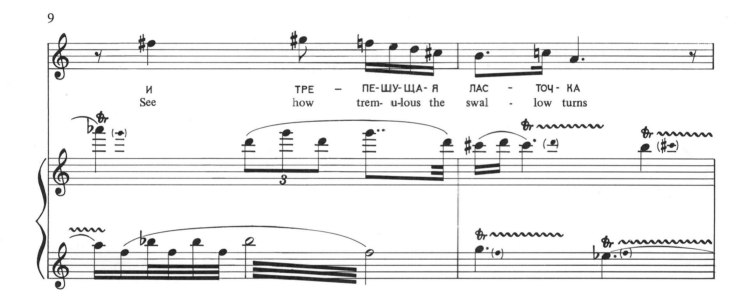

И ТРЕ - ПЕ - ШУ-ЩА-Я ЛАС - ТОЧ - КА
See how trem- u-lous the swal - low turns

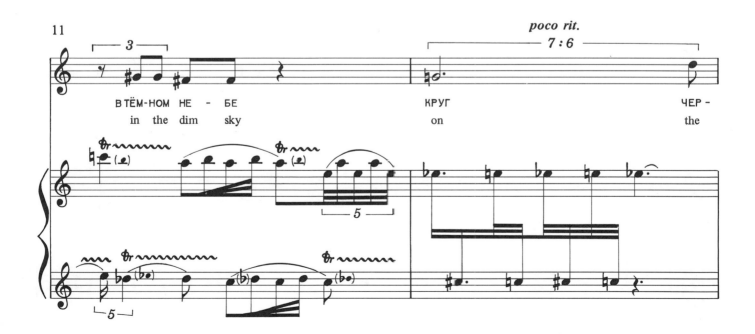

poco rit.

7 : 6

В ТЁМ-НОМ НЕ - БЕ КРУГ ЧЕР -
in the dim sky on the

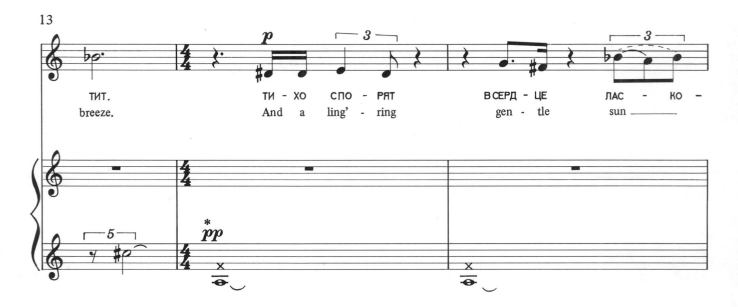

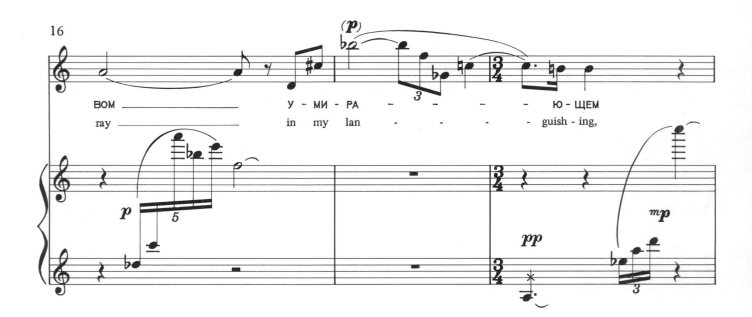

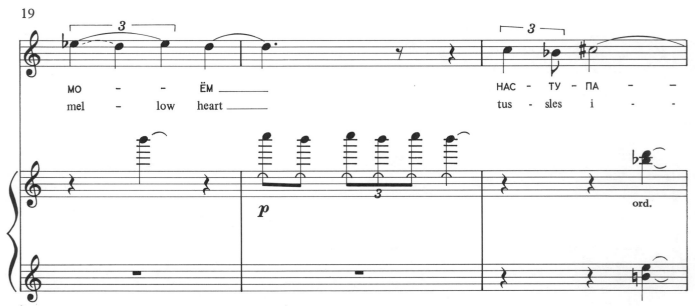

* Insert a small screw between the strings to give a bell - like sound.

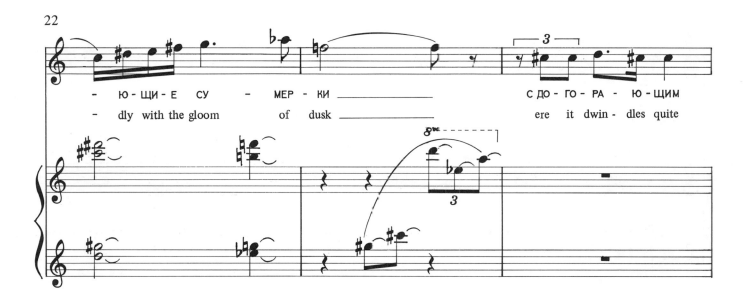

- Ю - ЩИ-Е СУ - МЕР - КИ _____ С ДО - ГО - РА - Ю-ЩИМ
- dly with the gloom of dusk _____ ere it dwin - dles quite

Tempo I

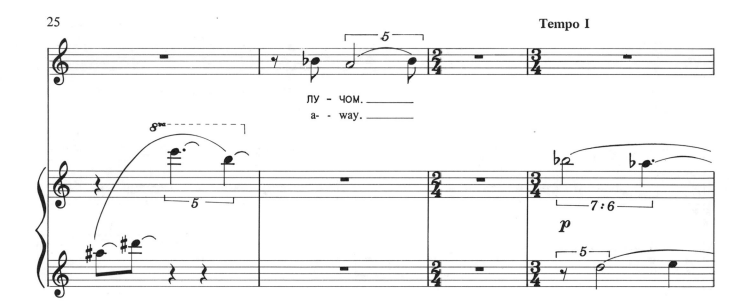

ЛУ - ЧОМ. _____
a- - way. _____

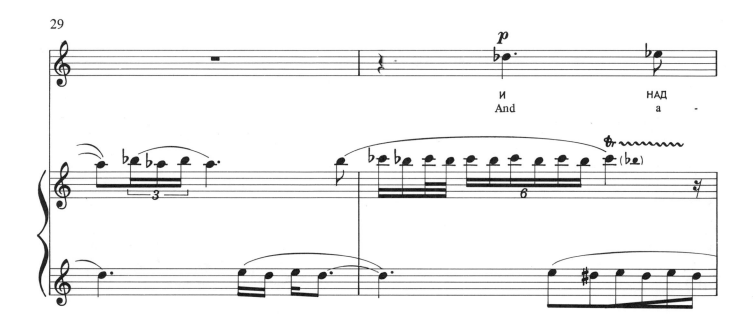

И НАД
And a -

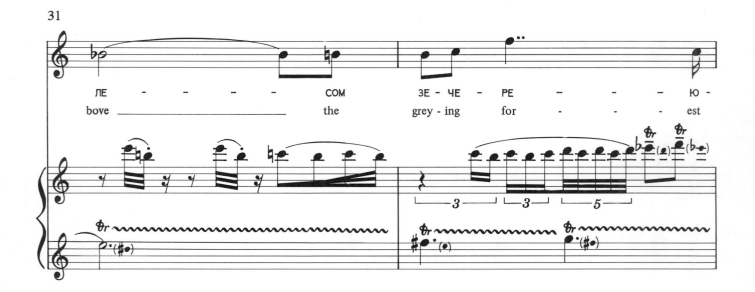

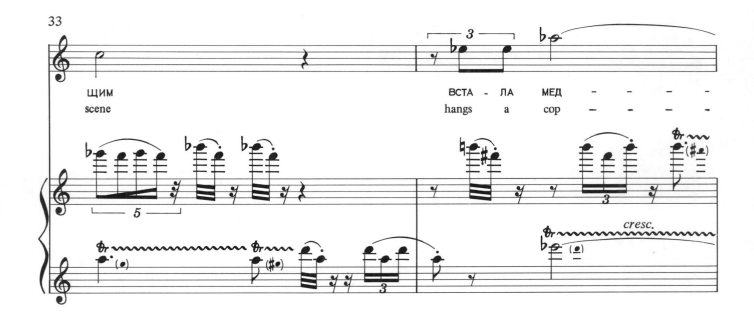

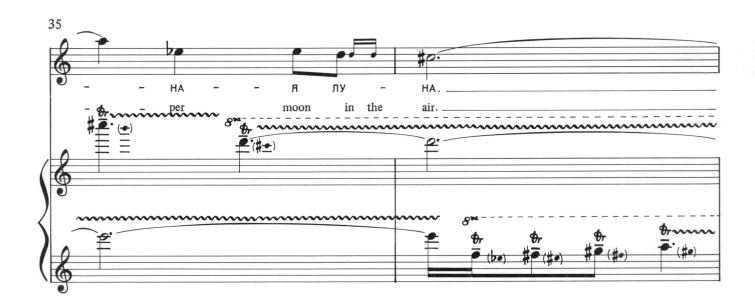

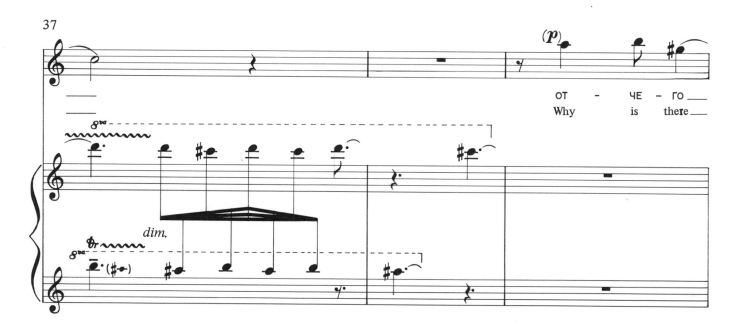

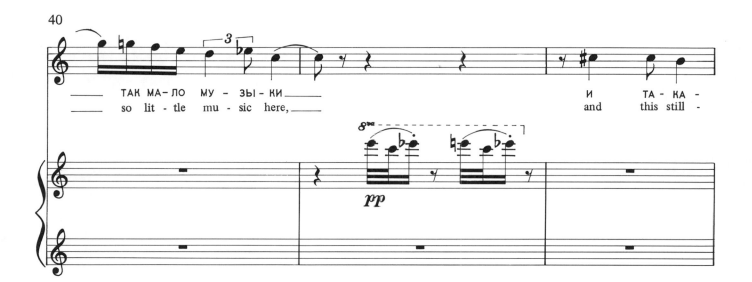

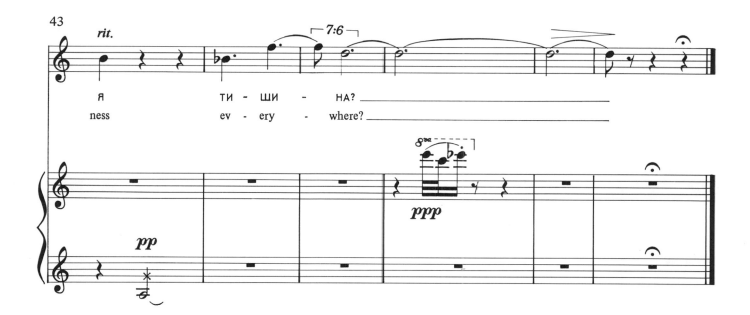